"You can't get the right answers without asking the right questions. In this book Pat teaches you the right questions to ask and where to find the best answers. Read this then go live it."

Andy Traub, Author of The Early To Rise Experience

TakePermission.com

"God's will is always the right decision...If you're someone who want's to make the right decisions yet you struggle with knowing God's will, this book is the key that will unlock your confusion. With God's Word as his guide, Pastor Pat provides a powerful perspective on how to intuitively and experientially know the will of God."

Dan Hickling, Web Pastor, Calvary Chapel of Fort Lauderdale

Calvaryftl.org

"Huge things come in small packages. Don't let its brevity fool you. Pastor Pat Sieler's little book, Direction: Discovering & Living the Will of God, does an awesome job of answering what may be the most important question that people ask. Not only will you love this book, but you will love to refer back to it over and over again."

Daniel Fusco, Lead Pastor, Crossroads Community Church

www.crossroadschurch.net - www.danielfusco.com

Direction: Discovering & Living the Will of God

PAT SIELER

ISBN: 9781709970757

All Greek definitions are taken from J. Strong,
Enhanced Strong's Lexicon. Bellingham, WA:
Logos Bible Software, 2001.

DEDICATION

Dedicated to my wife, Janet Marie,
and my kids, Genesis Faith, Caleb Elijah, and Levi Lucas.
I love discovering and living God's will with you!

CONTENTS

Preface		1
Chapter 1	The Big Picture	3
Chapter 2	What Does the Bible Say?	9
Chapter 3	Three Tools to Determine Divine Direction	17
Chapter 4	Tool #1: Spiritual Impressions	23
Chapter 5	What About Visions and Dreams?	29
Chapter 6	Tool #2: Spiritual Insight	35
Chapter 7	Tool #3: Spiritual Intentions	41
Extras	Downloads	45
Appendix 1	The Worksheets	47
Worksheet A	Brainstorming Your Life: 25 Questions to Help You See the Big Picture	49
Worksheet B	Living Biblically	59
Worksheet C	Using the Tools	63
Appendix 2	Selected Scriptures	71

PREFACE

I am a pastor. Like any pastor, I care about people. I realized a long time ago that the mission of my life is to help people grow closer to Jesus. That's what I want to be about, and that's the reason for this book: I'm writing it because the people I have a special charge to give spiritual nurture and care to, those whom God has placed under my trust, those who want to be closer to Jesus, have a desire to know and do His will.

This only makes sense. We call ourselves *Christians*; we are followers of Jesus Christ. That means He is our leader. As our leader, certainly He has specific desires and plans for each one of us. Yet, as I'm sure you've experienced, life is full of choices— many of them very important choices. Which ones should we choose? How do we evaluate the options before us? After all, as Christians we recognize that we are not living primarily for our own pleasure or success in this life on earth, but rather to please Him. As David Watson said, "To obey God's will is to find the fulfillment of our lives."

Direction: Discovering and Living the Will of God is not meant to be a comprehensive treatise on the subject of God's will. It certainly is not all that will ever be said about this subject! My intention is not to provide academic study material. Rather, on the pages that follow, you will find what I would share with you if we were able to get together for a cup of coffee and you asked for some help in making an important decision. I have attempted to make it brief enough that the material can be worked through in a relatively short amount of time, perhaps less than a week. It is meant to be an aid to your Bible study and a tool to help you pray and think about what God has for you. (See especially the worksheets at the back of the book.)

My earnest prayer is that after prayerfully reading through *Direction: Discovering and Living the Will of God*, you will find yourself closer to Jesus.

Until we meet,

Pastor Pat Sieler

"All heaven is waiting to help those who will discover the will of God and do it."
~ J. Robert Ashcroft

CHAPTER 1
THE BIG PICTURE

"What is God's will for my life?"

It is one question that all of us who name the name of Christ have asked at some point in our lives.

"Should I go here or should I go there?"

"Should I go to this school . . . take this job . . . marry this person . . . move to this city?"

I've known many people who have struggled with the decision of whether or not to quit their job and "go into the ministry." An even bigger consideration is, "Who should I marry?"

Whether educational, vocational, matrimonial, or geographical choices, we all have to make them at some point. We all want to make the right decisions. But how do we know if our decision will be the right one? What if we blow it? What if we make the wrong decision in one of these important areas?

Sometimes people wonder if they are living life "outside the will of God." How can you be sure that you are in God's will? Have you ever wondered if God even has a will?

Could it be that we are asking the wrong question?

The Bigger Question

Let's do something that is hard for those of us who live in North America. Let's forget about ourselves! Let's not ask the question, "What is God's will for my life?" and let's ask the question, "What is God's will for the world?"

Aaah! Now we are on to something!

God's plan for the world can be summarized in two words: salvation and discipleship. God wants people to be saved (1 Timothy 2:4). After they are saved, He wants them to become growing Christians (Colossians 2:6–7, Matthew 28:19–20).

Did not Jesus come to provide a way for us to be saved? Is this not absolutely the most important message in the history of the world?

Once a man, woman, boy, or girl experiences salvation, God's plan for that individual is spiritual growth. He wants each of us to become mature in faith. He does not want us to be stagnant but to be growing.

In fact, the writer of the letter to the Hebrews assumed that spiritual growth was the expected norm of Christians. He expected the readers of the letter not just to be growing, but to be becoming teachers: "Although by this time you ought to be teachers . . ."

(Hebrews 5:12).

So let's take this question of God's will for our lives a step further. If God is all about evangelism and discipleship, doesn't it make sense that His will for your life and mine would have something to do with those two purposes? Instead of asking, "What is God's will for my life?", perhaps the better question is, "How am I uniquely equipped to invest my time, talents, and treasures to be part of fulfilling God's will (evangelism and discipleship) for the world?"

More Questions

If you are a Christian, God's will for your life has something to do with evangelism and discipleship.

Keeping that as the foundation, start asking yourself questions like this: "What am I good at? What do I do that blesses other people? What do I want to do before I die? How am I using my disposable income? What gets me more excited: evangelism or discipleship? What have I done that God has really blessed? What opportunities do I have that others don't? If money was no object, what would I do? Where would I go?"

What about your current career? Does your job open up any opportunities for you to take the love of Jesus to places where there is no witness for Christ? Will that increase in salary give you more financial resources to help missionaries or sponsor a new evangelism program at your church?

Single? Does the person you are dating help you grow closer to Jesus? Is your future spouse ministry minded? If not, do not marry that person!

Have you considered starting a Bible study or prayer group in your new school or neighborhood?

Do you love to travel and learn about other cultures? What about taking your skills to countries that are closed to the gospel?

Have you ever considered mentoring younger men or women? Do you have ministry experience or life skills from which others could learn?

Stop reading for a moment. Pray. Then go back through this list of questions, and take some time to write down some answers. Do some soul-searching, keeping in mind that God is all about evangelism and discipleship. When you truly understand what is on God's heart, you will make different choices.

It's not just about choosing a job or a school or a mate. It's about examining that decision in light of God's master plan of evangelism and discipleship.

One of the reasons I decided to become a senior pastor is for this very matter. Over time, I began to see that the best way for me to fulfill the Great Commission in my life was to pastor a church.

That's not going to be the same for you, necessarily. But you are called by God to do something in the way of discipling others. If you are not making disciples, you are out of the will of God. God wants to use your life to help others grow closer to Him.

It may happen as you start a lunchtime prayer meeting or Bible study at work. It may happen as you open your home to host a small group from your church. It may be sharing your testimony with a coworker or at a business luncheon. If you are a plumber or a carpet cleaner, when you go into a customer's house, are you open to sharing the love of

Jesus with that customer? Do you pray for them, if only quietly to yourself?

If you have children, you have a God-given mandate to disciple them. If you don't have children, whenever you interact with younger people at your church, encourage them in the things of the Lord.

Whether it's formal discipleship and mentoring, or whether it's informally but intentionally talking about God with people, you are a disciple maker and a soul winner!

You are part of God's plan for the world. You can do this today!

"The fundamental mode whereby our rational Creator guides his rational creatures is by rational understanding and application of his written Word."
~ J.I. Packer

CHAPTER 2
WHAT DOES THE BIBLE SAY?

The most important activity to help us discover God's will is spending time in prayerful reading of God's Word.

It is true that as we read His Word, sometimes a verse seems to jump off the page and address a particular issue or situation that we are going through. It leaves an impression on our minds and our hearts. These can be significant experiences; God certainly uses His Word to speak to us in this way.

When I was praying about pastoring the Calvary Chapel church in Oakville, Ontario, Canada, I believe God spoke to me many times through His written

Word.

When I was praying about marrying my wife, Janet, I believe God spoke to me through several Bible verses over the course of many months during my times of devotion and prayer.

These were times of spiritual confirmation and direction. They were significant occasions in my life. Because of the input of God's Word during these prayerful times, I was able to move forward with confidence.

If you are reading this book, it may be that you are praying about a big decision. If you don't know what to do about a certain issue, ask God to speak to you through His Word. I believe He will.

But above and beyond these types of spiritual impressions that help us make decisions about our lives, there are several facets of God's will for everyone that are clearly revealed in the Bible.

God's Will Revealed

We often want to know if it is God's will to go to this school, or to take this job, or to start this business. Those are all important issues, and God is concerned about them. However, the spiritual impressions we sometimes receive about these situations can be somewhat subjective.

One of the most important lessons I've learned is that the more critical aspect of God's will is what He has clearly revealed in Scripture. There are several statements in the New Testament that have to do with God's will. They all have more to do with who you are than where you are.

In other words, God is more concerned about your

character and your attitude than your geographical location or vocation.

Let's look at some of these verses that make God's will very, very clear.

The first tells us that God's will is your holiness.

Sanctification

> For this is God's will, your sanctification: that you abstain from sexual immorality, so that each of you knows how to control his own body in sanctification and honor, not with lustful desires, like the Gentiles who don't know God. This means one must not transgress against and defraud his brother in this matter, because the Lord is an avenger of all these offenses, as we also previously told and warned you. (1 Thessalonians 4:3–6)

Do you want to know what God's will is? It's your sanctification. Sanctification means to be set apart. God's will is for you to live a holy, separated life—not in a monastery, but separate from the over-sexualized culture of the world today. He wants you to be pure. That's God's will!

You don't have to pray what He wants for your life in this area! Just pray to be able to live it out!

It is not God's will for you to watch pornography, sleep with your girlfriend or boyfriend, fantasize, or lust.

When it comes to determining God's will in your life, start there. Make sure you are living out 1 Thessalonians 4:3–6 before you pray about what car or laptop to buy!

Transformation

God's Word also teaches us that we can only know His will as we are transformed by Him. This is an important principle. If you do not want to spend time in prayer and in the Word so that your thinking is renewed, discovering God's will is going to be impossible.

Do not be conformed to this age, but be transformed by the renewing of your mind, so that you may discern what is the good, pleasing, and perfect will of God. (Romans 12:2)

The more we spend time with Jesus, the more we get to know Him. The more we know Him, the more we love Him. The more we love Him, the more we will start thinking like Him. The more we think like Him, the more we will understand what His will is.

This is true for the child and the parent. If my eight-year-old son never spends time with me, he will never know my will. He will never be able to think like me.

God's will, for each one of us, will always be our spiritual growth and transformation. As I spend time with Jesus, doing His will becomes a natural outgrowth of my relationship with Him.

My kids don't run around and ask each other what Dad's will is for their life. If they just hang out with me, they will get to the right place.

It's all about relationship: a true relationship with God will lead to my continual transformation.

Spiritual Vitality

"Rejoice always! Pray constantly. Give thanks in

everything, for this is God's will for you in Christ Jesus." (1 Thessalonians 5:16–18)

Constant joy, constant prayer, and constant gratitude is God's will for each and every one of us. Joy, prayer, and thankfulness are three simple measuring sticks that we can use to gauge our walk with the Lord.

Do you have joy in your life? How much time are you spending in prayer? What's on your gratitude list?

God's will is not just an agenda or an itinerary. Give some time every day to these three components of your life. Rejoice, pray, and be thankful. If you do that, you will be right in the middle of God's will!

Do What You Know

Samuel Annesley, John Wesley's father-in-law, said, "Do what you know, and God will teach you what to do. Do what you know to be your present duty, and God will acquaint you with your future duty as it comes to be present."

Your present duty? Sanctification, transformation, and spiritual vitality. Focus on those realities, and it could be that every other decision will become much more clear.

Oh, one more thing. I almost forgot!

Suffering

"For it is better, if it is the will of God, to suffer for doing good than for doing evil." (1 Peter 3:17)

Sometimes it's God's will for you to suffer. There, I said it.

I know it's not a really popular message. In fact,

there's a whole camp of Christianity that says, "It is God's will for you to be healthy and wealthy. If you're not healthy, there is sin in your life; if you're not wealthy, you don't have enough faith."

My wife and I lived many years in Miami, Florida. Whenever we would drive to my mother-in-law's house in Little Havana, we would pass by several Hispanic churches. One of them always had a sign out front that said "Pare de Sufrir" (Stop Suffering).

I never walked into that church or heard a message from their pastor, but assuming they really preach that as Christians we should not suffer, they are preaching heresy. It is just not true. In fact, the entire book of 1 Peter was written to encourage Christians who were going through suffering. The gospel that says God doesn't want us to suffer is a false gospel.

On the contrary, sometimes it is God's will that we suffer. If we suffer because of a mistake we made or a sin we committed, we can't blame that on God. That's our own fault.

But when we do good, when we are trying to please the Lord and suffering comes our way, it certainly does not mean that we are out of God's will.

In fact, suffering is one of the great tools that God uses to mold our character. It is through the crucible of suffering that we are made more sensitive to His Spirit and more attentive to His Word.

An old Puritan minister from the seventeenth century, Richard Baxter, said "Suffering so unbolts the door of the heart that the Word hath easier entrance."

Trials tune our heart to the key of God's voice. They reveal the true depth of our spirituality and make us aware of our frailty and need for Jesus.

We all know people who have gone through terrible and not-so-terrible suffering and have had amazing times of ministry.

Years ago, I knew some guys who had a pretty good Christian band, named 360-Zip, as I recall. The lead singer, Phil, had to undergo a routine tonsillectomy. Something went wrong during the procedure, and if I remember correctly, he lost a lot of blood and almost lost his life.

He shared his testimony about that experience in church on a Sunday shortly following. Here's part of what he said: "If it would bring God glory, I would be willing to go through all of that again."

I never forgot that.

If it is God's will for you to suffer, rejoice. He will carry you through.

"God's heavenly plan doesn't always make
earthly sense."
~ Charles Swindoll

CHAPTER 3
THREE TOOLS TO DETERMINE
DIVINE DIRECTION

So far, we have learned that God's will for our lives must have something to do with evangelism and discipleship. We have also learned that the Bible is very clear that God's will has much to do with our character and maturity, above and beyond our career, school, or choice of marriage partner.

Nonetheless, we all, from time to time, find ourselves in situations where we are faced with choices. We want to make the right choice. So how do we do it?

How Did Paul Do It?

The book of Acts is an important book in the Bible because it traces the growth of the church from a small group of 120 Jewish followers of Jesus meeting in an upper room in Jerusalem to a very large, perhaps innumerable group of disciples all over Judea, Samaria, and into the western world.

I wonder if those in the early church wrestled with knowing God's will as much as we do today. They certainly lived His will—at least, many whose stories we know did.

The apostle Paul is one such man. He was used by God to take the gospel message throughout the areas of what we know as Turkey, Greece, and into Europe. Certainly he must have been in the centre of God's will!

Acts 16:6–13 is a passage that has to do with Paul and his team discovering God's will—and obeying it!

In this passage, Paul and his companions, Silas and Timothy, are traversing the land, getting ready to forge ahead into new territories. But something happens. They change their course as the Spirit of God redirects their steps. They want to go one way, but God leads them to go a different way. It's divine direction!

Many of our decisions and questions about God's will have to do with change, often geographical change. While it is not wise to determine doctrine from historical narrative, it is instructional to see how God worked in the lives of our brothers and sisters who were part of the early church and whose lives the Holy Spirit decided to record in the Bible. Remember, the apostle Paul and all those we read about in Scripture were human too!

Let's take a look at the passage:

> They went through the region of Phrygia and Galatia and were prevented by the Holy Spirit from speaking the message in Asia. When they came to Mysia, they tried to go into Bithynia, but the Spirit of Jesus did not allow them. So, bypassing Mysia, they came down to Troas. During the night a vision appeared to Paul: A Macedonian man was standing and pleading with him, "Cross over to Macedonia and help us!" After he had seen the vision, we immediately made efforts to set out for Macedonia, concluding that God had called us to evangelize them. Then, setting sail from Troas, we ran a straight course to Samothrace, the next day to Neapolis, and from there to Philippi, a Roman colony, which is a leading city of that district of Macedonia. We stayed in that city for a number of days. On the Sabbath day we went outside the city gate by the river, where we thought there was a place of prayer. We sat down and spoke to the women gathered there. (Acts 16:6–13)

Did you notice all the geographical names: Phrygia, Galatia, Asia, Mysia, Bithynia, Troas, Macedonia, Samothrace, Neapolis, Philippi?

Eight verses, ten locations! There's some movement going on here!

Previously, Paul and his team were spending time with the Christians in Galatia. (Galatia was a region much like a province. It wasn't a city.) Paul had been used by God to plant several churches in Galatia a few years earlier. The purpose of this trip in Acts 16 was to encourage the believers in these churches and see how they were doing.

As that phase of their trip came to a close, evidently they decided to go to Asia. This was not the modern Asia that we think of, but a small province where Ephesus was located, in southern Turkey bordering on the Mediterranean Sea.

Forbidden by the Holy Spirit

As they tried to go to this area, Acts 16:6 says that they were "prevented by the Holy Spirit." Hmmm? What does that mean: "prevented by the Holy Spirit"?

Something must have happened that kept them from going southwest. So they try to go northeast into this area called Bithynia, which is also in modern-day Turkey south of the Black Sea. Again, the Word of God tells us, "The Spirit of Jesus did not allow them" (Acts 16:7).

They try to go left, God says no.

They try to go right, God says no.

The Bible clearly says that the Spirit prevented them from going in a certain direction. Finally, they decided to go an entirely new direction.

As we examine what really happened in these verses, we see Paul, Silas, and Timothy using three "tools" to discover what God would have them do. We can use them too. They are impressions, insight, and intentions.

One caution here. These tools cannot be used individually; they must be used collectively.

Impressions + insight + intentions = living God's will.

Let's look at each one.

"The life of the believer is a conducted tour, and the skillful guide is Abraham's guide and ours. He knows the end of the journey which is in view, and he knows the best way to arrive there."
~ Fred Mitchell

CHAPTER 4
TOOL #1: SPIRITUAL IMPRESSIONS

"They were prevented by the Holy Spirit." "The Spirit of Jesus did not allow them . . ."

It sounds pretty significant, pretty strong. The King James Version says, "They were forbidden by the Holy Spirit."

I don't think we are talking about a "hunch," a fanciful whim, or a fleeting thought. That's not the kind of impression happening to these missionaries. I believe Paul and his party had a very significant spiritual impression not to go a certain direction. They were restrained by Jesus. The door they wanted to go through, Asia, was closed. They tried another door, and that door too was closed.

But what do we mean by a "closed" door? How, exactly, did these "impressions" happen? There are a couple of possibilities.

Closed Doors

The closed door could have been circumstantial. It could have been that as they were traveling, they simply ran into some type of hardship, perhaps a horrible illness.

If you were driving your car one direction and you ran into a roadblock or got a flat tire, that would be a circumstantial closed door. God sometimes leads us through circumstances.

If it wasn't circumstantial, the closed door could have been a lack of peace. I think this is more likely.

I imagine that as they tried to go into these different areas, something just didn't feel right. They knew somehow, through a lack of peace in their hearts, that God was not calling them to that particular region.

In my experience, this is how the Lord often leads us. The apostle Paul wrote, "Let the peace of God rule in your hearts" (Colossians 3:15, KJV).

The word "rule" in this verse is translated from the Greek word brabeuo, which means "to be an umpire, to determine, to decide."

This is huge! A spiritual impression can be a lack of the peace from God about a certain situation or direction.

During your decision making process, ask yourself

these questions: "If I say yes to this opportunity, will I have peace? What will happen if I say no? Would that give me a greater peace?"

In other words, as you consider the consequence of living with the decision you are about to make, do you have peace about it? Or a lack of peace? Let the peace of Christ be the umpire of your decisions.

Away from the Need

Whatever the closed door was for Paul and his team, whether circumstances or a lack of peace or both, I find it fascinating that God directed them not to go to a place where there was a need.

Think about that! The people to the south and the north needed the gospel. But God told Paul no. He closed the door.

Why?

It simply wasn't His will. God had other plans.

God did eventually open the door for the gospel to be preached in Bithynia and this province called Asia. We know that because the apostle Peter wrote a letter to the believers who lived there! First Peter 1:1 says, "Peter, an apostle of Jesus Christ, to the strangers scattered throughout Pontus, Galatia, Cappadocia, Asia, and Bithynia" (KJV).

Paul and Silas and Timothy were not the right people. It was not the right time. Maybe God called Peter to go there instead.

In his Expositions of Holy Scripture: the Acts, one of my favorite Bible commentators, Alexander Maclaren, writes "Christ himself directs the expansion of his kingdom."

We don't know why Christ chose who He chose

for what He chose or when He chose! But He did choose! He chose you for what you are doing, and He chose me for what I am doing. He is the great conductor. As 1 Corinthians 12:18 says, "But now God has placed each one of the parts in one body just as He wanted" (1 Corinthians 12:18, emphasis mine).

There are many legitimate, even heartbreaking needs in the world today. But the existence of a need does not, in and of itself, constitute a calling from the Lord to meet that need. It must be said, though, that an awareness of a need may be the beginning of a call. As a burden grows, a calling may mature out of it.

An Open Door

A lack of peace is one spiritual impression that we can have. A second type of impression is what I call a "stirred heart." This often happens when we see an opportunity, our hearts are stirred with excitement, and we want to take a venture of faith!

When it comes to ventures of faith, I always think about a certain event in the life of Jonathan, King Saul's son. His heart was stirred to go see what was going on in the camp of the Philistines, the Israelites' enemy. His words to his armor-bearer say it all:

"And Jonathan said to the young man that bare his armor, Come, and let us go over unto the garrison of these uncircumcised: it may be that the Lord will work for us: for there is no restraint to the Lord to save by many or by few." (1 Samuel 14:6, KJV)

Jonathan saw an opportunity, grabbed a brother, and tested the waters. The result was a major victory for the Israelites and for the Lord.

Jonathan responded to the impression in his excited

heart in three ways.

First, he told someone close to him, someone he trusted. If your heart is stirred to take on a new project, begin a ministry, or launch some other venture of faith, tell someone you trust. See what they think. (We'll cover this more in the chapter on insight.)

Second, he tested the waters. Jonathan did not rush into his decision presumptuously. He took a little step of faith to see if God was in it. He was. Jonathan knew at that point that he would meet with success. The stirring in his heart was colliding with an incredible opportunity!

Third, he went for it! He allowed his dream to be lived out. He was accomplishing something for God. No doubt he was nervous, but he did not allow his fears to cripple him.

A stirred heart, an encouraging brother, and an amazing opportunity. That's a venture of faith.

But it started with a simple impression from the Lord in the heart of one of His servants.

"Men give advice; God gives guidance."
~ Leonard Ravenhill

CHAPTER 5
WHAT ABOUT VISIONS AND DREAMS?

Paul, Silas and Timothy experienced two closed doors: one to the south and one to the north. The only natural option now seems to be to go west. So they head to a city called Troas, on the coast of the Aegean Sea.

At night, Paul receives a vision of a man from Macedonia asking for help. This was the confirmation that they needed to take the gospel west.

During the night a vision appeared to Paul: A Macedonian man was standing and pleading with him, "Cross over to Macedonia and help us!" (Acts 16:9)

Visions Today?

God gave Paul a vision. That vision proved very significant in their decision to head toward Philippi. In fact, one wonders if they would have continued west without it.

But how does this apply to our decision-making process? Does God still give visions today? In determining God's will, what role should supernatural experiences, such as visions or dreams, play?

One of my pastor friends recommended that I meet with a young lady named Devorah. She had just moved from his town to the area where I was pastoring. He wanted me to hear her story and learn about her ministry. She works for the Canadian Centre for Bioethical Reform, an organization committed to ending abortion. After hearing her story, I asked her to send me her written testimony. Here it is:

> When I was thirteen years old, I had a dream. Actually, it was a nightmare! I was walking with my friends, goofing off and having fun. Then I stepped on something and heard a sickening crunch underneath my foot. I jumped back to see what I had stepped on. It was a little girl, bloody, somewhat mangled, and dead. My friends and I gasped absolutely horrified at what we saw. Then we looked up. As far as the eye could see in every direction we were surrounded by children—boys and girls, bloody, somewhat mangled, all of them dead. Then I heard a voice: "This is your generation. These are the children that have been aborted. I have heard their blood cry out to me. If you do nothing, their blood will be on your heads." Then I woke up.

Devorah had a dream that changed her life. Today, she is busy changing the world for many others.

God certainly can use visions and dreams to speak to us. He can also certainly use a word of wisdom or a word of knowledge or a prophecy from another brother or sister.

Years ago, I was at an early morning prayer meeting with some leaders from the church I was attending. We laid hands on one particular brother because he was getting ready to start a church in a community south of where we were meeting.

As we were praying, I sensed that the Lord was giving me a word for him. It was something like, "I have appointed you to speak to the nations." Now, this type of impression doesn't come to me every time we pray. But this was one of those times that I really sensed it was the Lord and I needed to share it with him. So I did.

At the time, he was a young, passionate, newly married man who, like the rest of us, didn't know much about pastoring, let alone planting a church. But over the years, the church this brother started has experienced tremendous growth. He also has spoken at many pastors' conferences all over the United States and in other countries.

Spiritual Sensitivity

I believe that being sensitive to the voice of the Lord is critical in walking with Jesus, especially in times of decision making. But it is even more critical that we test all things with the written Word of God.

If you receive a vision, prophecy, word of knowledge or the like, that you believe is from God, here are three steps you need to take before acting on it.

1. *Test it by the Word of God.*

We certainly cannot put more faith in the words of men and women than in the written Word of God. God will never, ever ask or tell you to do something that is contrary to His written Word. Ever.

He will never ask you to rob a bank or beat your wife. If you are contemplating doing anything like that, you are out of God's will and need to repent and seek counsel!

I knew of a young lady who was leaving her husband for another man. All involved parties were supposedly Christian. When a godly sister and friend approached this young lady to bring some accountability and much needed correction into her life, she responded, "When I married Mark [not his real name], I wasn't thinking clearly." And you are thinking clearly now? I thought when I heard this.

If she had submitted her life to the Word of God, she would not have made such a foolish choice. God's written Word always trumps our emotions, as well as our visions and dreams.

2. *Seek counsel from others.*

Proverbs 20:18 teaches us that "every purpose is established by counsel" (KJV). Especially in the big decisions of life, such as marriage and career changes, we need input from mature people who know and love us. This doesn't mean we will always do what they say, but godly counsel in invaluable. The objectivity of those who have no personal interest in the benefits of our decision may help us see additional benefits or consequences.

There should be someone in your life who is not afraid to ask you the tough questions. Allow them to poke at the depths of your soul and uncover any potential greed for power or money or status. Allow them to question your motivation. It will be good for you!

3. Pray seriously and diligently.

You are foolish if you make major decisions without prayer. That's a strong statement, but it's an important one.

Hebrews 4:16 teaches us that we have direct access to God's throne. It is the place where we receive grace and help. We personally know the sovereign Lord of all. As we pray, we submit our will to Him. It is through prayer that great things happen. Many times, an idea or an answer has come into my mind as I was praying about a matter.

These three steps are essential. I have had well-intentioned people tell me prophetic things that did not come to pass. When I was seventeen years old, a well-meaning lady told me that I would be married by the time I was twenty-two.

That's pretty awesome news for a young man with his whole life before him and a whole world of potential mates! Twenty-two came and went. No wife.

Twenty-three, twenty-four, twenty-five ... still single.

Would I be a bachelor till the rapture?!

I was thirty years old when I got married. Frankly, I never thought much about that prophecy in those days. I loved that lady who had shared the prophecy with me; God used her in my life in multiple ways. I am sure she sincerely thought she was hearing from the Lord. But had I taken her word as gospel truth and forced the issue of marriage when I was twenty-two, it could have been disastrous, to say the least!

Ultimately, you must do what you believe God has called you to do, not what someone else says God wants you to do.

Yes, God can speak today to you through visions and dreams. But His written Word is primary.

Submit your life to God's Word, seek good and godly counsel, and pray diligently.

"Wisdom and the will of God are intimately related . . . Nothing is more vital for practical knowledge of the purposes of God than wisdom."

~ Sinclair Ferguson

CHAPTER 6
TOOL #2: SPIRITUAL INSIGHT

The first tool we looked at for discovering the will of God was impressions. The second tool we can use to discern God's will for our lives is insight. Impressions, whether yours or others, come through prayer, reading God's Word, evaluating circumstances as we listen to the Spirit, and possibly, visions and dreams.

Insight is different; insight is wisdom.

Keep in mind, these tools are used together. Impressions must be combined with insight.

Listening to the Right People

Usually, wisdom comes with age. I know that's not always the case, but it should be.

One of my first wisdom experiences as an assistant pastor involved two interns. They were sitting in my office as we were going over the requirements of our new internship program. As I was talking to them about ministry, I noticed that what was coming out of my mouth sounded really wise! I was impressed!

I'm not trying to be a wise guy (pun intended), but what struck me about that conversation was that wisdom was naturally pouring out of my heart because of the years of experience I had.

For those major decisions in your life, it is wise to seek the counsel of men and women who have many more years of life under their belt than you do. They have learned something you don't yet know. Listen to their insight.

If only Rehoboam had done that! Second Chronicles 12 tells the story.

When King Solomon died, his son Rehoboam became king. A group of people came to King Rehoboam and said, "Your father put a heavy burden on us. Please lighten our load. If you do, we will serve you."

Rehoboam wisely went to his father's advisers, the older men, and asked them what he should do. They counseled him, "If you serve these people and speak good words to them, they will be your servants forever."

Golden advice.

But then Rehoboam went to the young men he had grown up with and said to them, "How should we answer these people who tell us to lighten their load?"

His friends told him, "Tell them, 'My little finger is thicker than my father's waist. I will make your yoke heavier.'"

That's exactly what he did.

He rejected the advice of the older, wiser men and took the advice of the younger men. He traded wise insight for pride and popularity.

It was that event which caused the people of God to split into two nations, the north and the south: ten tribes in the north became the nation of Israel, and two tribes in the south became the nation of Judah.

This turn of events was from the Lord, but it illustrates an important truth: sometimes what we want to do is motivated by our pride and desire for popularity. Grey-haired wisdom may bring that to light!

When making big choices, it's important to include the input of our friends and peers. But the insight of older, well-respected saints, when it is listened to, may save us much headache and heartbreak.

Knitting God's Will

After we have listened to the counsel of others we respect, both young and old, and have prayed and searched the Scriptures, it is time to arrive at a conclusion. That's what Paul and his crew did.

Now after he had seen the vision, immediately we sought to go to Macedonia, concluding that the Lord had called us to preach the gospel to them. (Acts 16:10, emphasis mine)

Let's take a look at this word "concluding." If you read this passage too fast, you might glance over its importance.

The Greek word for concluding means to "cause to coalesce, to put together in one's mind, to knit together, compare, or gather." Concluding means to take this and to take that and to knit it together. Concluding means to take all of the information you have gleaned about a particular situation, compare and contrast, and then draw a conclusion.

To put it briefly, it is exercising insight.

To draw a conclusion about God's will for your life is to take all the information He has revealed to you (through your impressions, your knowledge of His Word, the details about the circumstances, and the input of others who love and care about you) and knit them together.

The process of making an important decision is just that: a process. It takes time. As you "knit," God's will becomes clear.

God gave us a brain, and He is honored when we use it. He gave you the ability to reason and to think. It is good to put some thought into our different options, to consider pros and cons, to examine the input of those who know us well. Then, combining it all with prayer, draw a conclusion and go for it!

That's what Paul did. He looked at the closed doors and the vision, as well as (I'm sure) the opinions of those with him, their times of prayer and discussion, their sense of calling, and their knowledge of the heart of God. He and his companions put all of that together and came to a conclusion: God wants us to go to Macedonia!

Step on the Gas

When I was approaching high school graduation, I

faced a difficult decision. I had an opportunity to go on the road with a local Christian band that was really starting to gain some exposure and popularity. But I also had just been accepted to the University of Miami's Music Engineering program. To top it all off, my mom had recently passed away, and my dad had moved to a distant town in another state, so parental involvement during this critical period in my life was minimal.

After a church service one Sunday, I spoke with a man who offered to pray for me. As he was talking to me, he said a sentence that has stayed with me all these years: "You can't steer a car that isn't moving." His point was not to experience paralysis of analysis.

It is critically important to think through our major decisions using all the wisdom we have been given. It is important to seek counsel from godly people. It is important to pray and listen to the voice of God through His written Word. But there comes a time when we have to pull the trigger. We have to commit and just go for it.

Some decisions will always require faith.

It Just "Seems" Right

In Acts 15, when the early church was in the process of making a decision about how to deal with all the Gentiles coming to faith, they discussed and deliberated. Peter shared his experience; Paul and Barnabas shared their story. Finally, James responded with scriptural wisdom and validation of what God was doing. Then they came to a decision.

In their letter to the Gentile believers, they say how they arrived at that decision: "For it seemed good to the Holy Ghost, and to us, to lay upon you no greater burden than these necessary things" (Acts 15:28, KJV, emphasis mine)

It's as if they are saying, "We talked about it, we prayed about it, and it just seemed like the right thing to do."

That's not a bad way to discern direction. Pray about it, talk about it, then do what seems best.

It's using the spiritual insight given by God.

But there's one more tool.

"The will of God is not something we are just
to understand; it is something we are
to undertake."
~ G.B. Duncan

CHAPTER 7
TOOL #3: SPIRITUAL INTENTIONS

The third and final tool that God has given us to
discover His will is having the proper intention.

Obedience

"Therefore loosing from Troas, we came with a
straight course to Samothracia, and the next day to
Neapolis." (Acts 16:11, KJV)

What's the first word of Acts 16:11? Therefore.

"Because we had an impression of closed doors,
because Paul received a vision of a man pleading with
him, because we used our spiritual insight as we knit
everything together in forming our conclusion . . .
Therefore, We. Set. Sail."

We acted. We committed. We did it.

Here is the essential key for discovering the will of God: obedience. Say that word out loud: obedience.

Paul and his boys were willing to obey. They had the intention of obedience.

Are you willing to do the hard work of obedience?

Why should God show you what He wants you to do, if you are not going to do it?

If you are not willing to push the boat away from the dock, if you're not willing to raise the sail or pick up an oar and start paddling, God's not going to show you what boat to get on.

Paul, Silas, Timothy, and now Luke set sail. When they land, they get off the boat. They walk to Philippi. They go to a prayer meeting. They open their mouths for ministry.

It's action.

They've prayed, they've talked. Now it's time to do!

Are You Willing?

Are you willing to do what God wants you to do? Are you willing to lay aside your will for God's will?

It was our Savior Jesus Christ who gave us the model of having the right intentions. His greatest struggle was in the garden of Gethsemene, directly preceding His arrest, His mockery of a trial, and His brutal, bloody death.

The physical torture Jesus endured was minuscule compared to the spiritual torture. All of the weight of the world's sins were placed upon Him. Fully aware of what awaited Him, how did He pray?

Let's listen in.

Then Jesus came with them to a place called

Gethsemane, and He told the disciples, "Sit here while I go over there and pray." Taking along Peter and the two sons of Zebedee, He began to be sorrowful and deeply distressed. Then He said to them, "My soul is swallowed up in sorrow—to the point of death. Remain here and stay awake with Me." Going a little farther, He fell facedown and prayed, "My Father! If it is possible, let this cup pass from Me. Yet not as I will, but as You will." (Matthew 26:36–39)

Jesus, during His darkest night, prays, "Let this cup pass from Me." He is saying, "Father, if there is any other way that mankind can be saved outside of the cross, let it happen."

There's an old Christian song I heard in a church service many years ago. I don't remember the songwriter's name, but I never forgot the lyrics: "Not my will, but Thine be done. In these seven simple words the battle's won. It's the perfect prayer of God's anointed Son. Not my will but Thine be done." I still hear that song in my head every time I read those words.

This is the best prayer that can be uttered when it comes to knowing God's will. It is truly the Lord's prayer—and it should be ours as well.

Whatever decision you are facing, please make this your prayer: "Not my will, but Thine be done."

Your career? "Not my will, but Thine be done."

Your spouse? "Not my will, but Thine be done."

Your venture in faith? "Not my will, but Thine be done."

When all is said and done, the issue is surrender.

We are the Lord's slaves. We are on this planet to do His will. It is not about my will; it is about the will of my Father.

Dear brother or sister, remember that God loves you; He is your Father. Jesus died on the cross to forgive you and set you free.

He has a plan for your life. He has a plan to prosper you and not to harm you, to give you a hope and a future.

He who began a good work in you will be faithful to complete it.

Rest in that.

Trust Him.

Obey His calling on your life.

May you hear, on that great day when you cross the finish line, "Well done, my good and faithful servant. Enter into the joy of your Lord."

EXTRAS
DOWNLOADS

Following are worksheets to help you process the material that you have just read. For purchasing this book, you are entitled to download the worksheets in PDF format so that it will be easier to fill in the answers.

You are also entitled to a free audio version of the full book in mp3 format.

To download these worksheets in PDF format, go to:
https://patsieler.com/product/direction-discovering-living-the-will-of-god-the-worksheets/

To download the audio book, go to:
https://patsieler.com/product/direction-discovering-and-living-the-will-of-god-the-audio-book/

You will be taken to the CalvaryTalk resource store. Upon checkout, enter the coupon code WSGRATIS to receive both the PDF Worksheets and the audio book for free.

APPENDIX 1
THE WORKSHEETS

(Note: To download these worksheets in PDF format, go to https://patsieler.com/product/direction-discovering-living-the-will-of-god-the-worksheets/

You will taken to the CalvaryTalk Resource Store. Enter in the coupon code WSGRATIS to download them for free.)

WORKSHEET A
BRAINSTORMING YOUR LIFE: 25 QUESTIONS TO HELP YOU SEE THE BIG PICTURE

Answer these questions. Don't spend a lot of time on each one. Write down the first things that come to mind.

1. List as many of your skills and talents that you can (at least five). These can be anything that you are good at.

2. What do you enjoy doing? Write down the first things that come to mind.

3. Write down five (or more) things that you want to do before you die.

4. What do you buy with your disposable income?

5. What gets you more excited: evangelism or discipleship? Circle one.

6. Which are you better at: evangelism or discipleship? Circle one.

7. What have you done that God has really blessed?

8. What opportunities do you have that others don't?

9. What makes you different from other people?

10. If money was no object, what would you do? Where would you go?

11. Do you like your job? Yes or No

12. If you could do anything else, what would it be?

13. How can you use your current career to help make disciples or present the gospel?

14. How can your vocation tie into discipleship or evangelism?

15. Are you willing to move overseas?

16. Does your job open up any new opportunities to take the love of Jesus to places where there is little or no witness for Christ?

17. If you received a salary increase, would you consider using it to help missionaries or sponsor a new evangelism program at your church?

18. How else could you spend your money that would contribute to God's plan for the world?

19. If you are single, does the person you are dating help you grow closer to Jesus? Is he or she ministry minded?

20. What can you do together that will help advance God's kingdom?

21. Have you considered starting a Bible study or prayer group in your new school or neighbourhood?

22. Have you ever considered mentoring younger men or women?

23. Do you have ministry experience or life skills from which others could learn?

24. Write down the name of one or two younger people you could mentor, either formally or informally. (If you are male, only mentor a male; if you are female, only mentor a female.)

25. If you had to make the decision right now, what would you choose?

WORKSHEET B
LIVING BIBLICALLY

On a scale of 1-10, rate the following:

Your Sexual Purity

"For this is God's will, your sanctification: that you abstain from sexual immorality, so that each of you knows how to control his own body in sanctification and honor, not with lustful desires, like the Gentiles who don't know God. This means one must not transgress against and defraud his brother in this matter, because the Lord is an avenger of all these offenses, as we also previously told and warned you." (1 Thessalonians 4:3–6)

1 - living in sin

2 -

3 - struggling daily

4 -

5 - falling regularly

6 -

7 - occasional slip, but accountable

8 -

9 -

10 - victory

Your Time Alone with God

"Do not be conformed to this age, but be transformed by the renewing of your mind, so that you may discern what is the good, pleasing, and perfect will of God." (Romans 12:2)

1 - no prayer or Bible study

2 -

3 - once in a while

4 -

5 - at least 2-3 times a week

6 -

7 - 4-5 times a week

8 -

9 -

10 - spending time daily with the Lord

Your Spiritual Vitality

"Rejoice always! Pray constantly. Give thanks in everything, for this is God's will for you in Christ Jesus." (1 Thessalonians 5:16–18)

On a scale of one to ten, rate yourself:

Do you rejoice?

1 2 3 4 5 6 7 8 9 10

Do you pray constantly?

1 2 3 4 5 6 7 8 9 10

Is prayer your first recourse?

YES NO SOMETIMES

What's on your gratitude list?

How thankful are you?

1 2 3 4 5 6 7 8 9 10

WORKSHEET C
USING THE TOOLS

The decision I am trying to make is:

Write down your experience with any of the following. Make sure you are praying as you do this. (Include detail. This is just between you and the Lord.)

Impressions

Scripture passages that have spoken clearly to my situation or decision:

Are there closed doors (circumstantial)?

What are the open doors (circumstantial)?

On a scale of 1–10, how much peace do I have regarding making this decision?

Have you had any visions or dreams?

Impressions I have received from others:

Insights

List the people you have asked for help in making this decision. Make sure you have sought the input of older, wiser people, such as godly parents or spiritual leaders, as well as peers and friends. (If you are married, you obviously should seek your spouse's input!)

Name:

What they thought (Scripture and/or counsel they gave you, etc.):

Name:

What they thought (Scripture and/or counsel they gave you, etc.):

Name:

What they thought (Scripture and/or counsel they gave you, etc.):

After looking at all of your impressions and insights, what is your gut feeling about this decision? Ask God to confirm this decision, then go for it!

APPENDIX 2
SELECTED SCRIPTURE PASSAGES

This may be the most valuable section of this book. While this list does not contain all of the verses in the Bible that have to do with God's will (for that I would have to include the whole Bible!) it does contain some passages that have been a blessing in my life over the years.

Read through this list, and then look up any passages that intrigue you, and spend some time looking at the context. Do it with any open heart and I am sure that God will speak to you.

I have included space for you to write down any observations or thoughts; I have also included some of mine.

All of these verses are from the World English Bible (WEB) translation. Visit worldenglish.bible for more information.

Genesis 25:22
"The children struggled together within her. She said, 'If it is like this, why do I live?' She went to inquire of Yahweh."

This is a fascinating passage. Isaac prays for his wife because she is barren. The Lord blesses her with child, but there is a great jostling in her womb. So she prays and the Lord answers her. Read the Lord's answer in Genesis 25:23. She had no idea what a big deal her pregnancy was until she prayed!

1 Samuel 9:9
"(In earlier times in Israel, when a man went to inquire of God, he said, "Come! Let's go to the seer;" for he who is now called a prophet was before called a seer.)"

In this passage we see that people would look to others, namely prophets, or seers, to help them with their decision making. While we do have the Holy Spirit within us, it is always a good idea to go to others whom we respect for help and advice.

Thoughts? What do you learn about God's will from this passage?

1 Samuel 23:1-5

David was told, "Behold, the Philistines are fighting against Keilah, and are robbing the threshing floors." Therefore David inquired of Yahweh, saying, "Shall I go and strike these Philistines?" Yahweh said to David, "Go strike the Philistines, and save Keilah."

David's men said to him, "Behold, we are afraid here in Judah. How much more then if we go to Keilah against the armies of the Philistines?" Then David inquired of Yahweh yet again. Yahweh answered him, and said, "Arise, go down to Keilah; for I will deliver the Philistines into your hand." David and his men went to Keilah and fought with the Philistines, and brought away their livestock, and killed them with a great slaughter. So David saved the inhabitants of Keilah.

David is a great case study in seeking God. We know that he didn't always get it right. But I love the fact that in several passages we see him "inquiring of the Lord."

Read this passage one more time and write down what it teaches you about asking God for direction?

1 Kings 22:5, 7-8
"Jehoshaphat said to the king of Israel, 'Please inquire first for Yahweh's word.' But Jehoshaphat said, 'Isn't there here a prophet of Yahweh, that we may inquire of him?'...The king of Israel said to Jehoshaphat, 'There is yet one man by whom we may inquire of Yahweh, Micaiah the son of Imlah; but I hate him, for he does not prophesy good concerning me, but evil.' Jehoshaphat said, 'Don't let the king say so.'"

Sometimes we only want to hear God tell us something positive, a blessing. But we need to be open to His chastening and rebuke as well.

What do you learn about God's character from this passage? Maybe read it in your Bible for more context.

2 Kings 3:11
But Jehoshaphat said, "Isn't there a prophet of Yahweh here, that we may inquire of Yahweh by him?" One of the king of Israel's servants answered, "Elisha the son of Shaphat, who poured water on the hands of Elijah, is here."

Jehoshaphat seemed to have a heart to know God's will, don't you think?

2 Kings 8:8
The king said to Hazael, "Take a present in your hand, and go meet the man of God, and inquire of Yahweh by him, saying, 'Will I recover from this sickness?' "

Does God always provide direct answers to our questions?

2 Kings 22:13

"Go inquire of Yahweh for me, and for the people, and for all Judah, concerning the words of this book that is found; for great is Yahweh's wrath that is kindled against us, because our fathers have not listened to the words of this book, to do according to all that which is written concerning us."

I love this passage because it centers on "the Book". May we listen to the words of the book, the Bible, and seek to live according to it.

What does this passage teach you about God? About humanity?

Psalm 27:4

"One thing I have asked of Yahweh, that I will seek after: that I may dwell in Yahweh's house all the days of my life, to see Yahweh's beauty, and to inquire in his temple."

Oh the Psalms! There's no better book to fuel your worship! Enter into His presence and seek His face!

What does this passage teach about the relationship between worship and knowing His will?

Can you think of any other Psalms that would be helpful in this regard?

Jeremiah 29:11-14

"'For I know the thoughts that I think toward you,' says Yahweh, 'thoughts of peace, and not of evil, to give you hope and a future. You shall call on me, and you shall go and pray to me, and I will listen to you. You shall seek me and find me, when you search for me with all your heart. I will be found by you,' says Yahweh, 'and I will turn again your captivity, and I will gather you from all the nations, and from all the places where I have driven you, says Yahweh. I will bring you again to the place from where I caused you to be carried away captive.'"

This is a famous passage and one that I love. While we must be careful to understand the context of any passage we are looking at, there are many truths about the Lord conveyed in these verses that should encourage you greatly. For one, if you seek Him, you will find Him.

What else do you see here?

Mark 3:35
"For whoever does the will of God is my brother, my sister, and mother."

What does this verse teach you about God's will?

Romans 1:9-10
"For God is my witness, whom I serve in my spirit in the Good News of his Son, how unceasingly I make mention of you always in my prayers, requesting, if by any means now at last I may be prospered by the will of God to come to you."

Here is another great verse from Paul's pen about his relationship with prayer and the will of God.

Romans 12:2
"Don't be conformed to this world, but be transformed by the renewing of your mind, so that you may prove what is the good, well-pleasing, and perfect will of God."

This is simply a great principal for knowing and living God's will.

Romans 15:30-33
"Now I beg you, brothers, by our Lord Jesus Christ and by the love of the Spirit, that you strive together with me in your prayers to God for me, that I may be delivered from those who are disobedient in Judea, and that my service which I have for Jerusalem may be acceptable to the saints, that I may come to you in joy through the will of God, and together with you, find rest. Now the God of peace be with you all. Amen."

See my comment on Romans 1:9-10. It is true for this passage as well!

1 Corinthians 1:1
"Paul, called to be an apostle of Jesus Christ through the will of God, and our brother Sosthenes..."

2 Corinthians 1:1
"Paul, an apostle of Christ Jesus through the will of God, and Timothy our brother, to the assembly of God which is at Corinth, with all the saints who are in the whole of Achaia:"

Ephesians 1:1
"Paul, an apostle of Christ Jesus through the will of God, to the saints who are at Ephesus, and the faithful in Christ Jesus..."

2 Timothy 1:1
Paul, an apostle of Jesus Christ through the will of God, according to the promise of the life which is in Christ Jesus,

Paul was an apostle by the will of God. What are you by the will of God? Go ahead, write it below.

2 Corinthians 8:5
"This was not as we had expected, but first they gave their own selves to the Lord, and to us through the will of God."

As we have been learning, the will of God involves our entire lives. In a word, surrender! What do you need to give your life to?

Ephesians 6:6
"...not in the way of service only when eyes are on you, as men pleasers, but as servants of Christ, doing the will of God from the heart"

What does this verse teach you about the will of God?

Philippians 2:12-14
"So then, my beloved, even as you have always obeyed, not only in my presence, but now much more in my absence, work out your own salvation with fear and trembling. For it is God who works in you both to will and to work, for his good pleasure. Do all things without complaining and arguing"

I love this passage! It teaches me that God is working in me! So encouraging! By the way, this verse does not mean that we have to work for our salvation. And I thought I'd include verse 14, do all things without complaining and arguing, just for fun. You're welcome.

Colossians 1:9-14

"For this cause, we also, since the day we heard this, don't cease praying and making requests for you, that you may be filled with the knowledge of his will in all spiritual wisdom and understanding, that you may walk worthily of the Lord, to please him in all respects, bearing fruit in every good work and increasing in the knowledge of God, strengthened with all power, according to the might of his glory, for all endurance and perseverance with joy, giving thanks to the Father, who made us fit to be partakers of the inheritance of the saints in light, who delivered us out of the power of darkness, and translated us into the Kingdom of the Son of his love, in whom we have our redemption, the forgiveness of our sins."

This is so rich! It is one of my favorite passages. You can use this to pray for yourself and others. Write your thoughts below.

Colossians 4:12

"Epaphras, who is one of you, a servant of Christ, salutes you, always striving for you in his prayers, that you may stand perfect and complete in all the will of God."

Spend some time thinking prayerfully about this passage. It connects God's will with prayer. Jot down your observations.

1 Thessalonians 4:3

"For this is the will of God: your sanctification, that you abstain from sexual immorality..."

1 Thessalonians 5:18

"In everything give thanks, for this is the will of God in Christ Jesus toward you."

We already looked at these, but they are listed here for your reference.

Hebrews 10:36
For you need endurance so that, having done the will of God, you may receive the promise.

I'm learning that perseverance is often God's will. Sometimes, we need to retreat or rest, but many times we are called to persevere. What's going on in your life right now that requires perseverance?

1 Peter 2:15
For this is the will of God, that by well-doing you should put to silence the ignorance of foolish men.

God wants us to do good deeds? We've all heard that actions speak louder than words. I'm not sure that's always true, but God always wants us to do good.

1 Peter 4:2
"that you no longer should live the rest of your time in the flesh for the lusts of men, but for the will of God."

The lust of men is never the will of God. What can you learn from this passage? Jot it down.

1 Peter 4:19
Therefore let them also who suffer according to the will of God in doing good entrust their souls to him, as to a faithful Creator.

ABOUT THE AUTHOR

Pat Sieler was born in Seattle, Washington, but spent most of his childhood in Las Vegas, Nevada, where he met Jesus when he was a teenager. He studied at University of Miami, Florida; Calvary Chapel Bible Institute in Fort Lauderdale, Florida; and Western Seminary in Portland, Oregon.

He has worked many years as a professional sound engineer and has served as an assistant pastor and worship leader, at both small and large churches. He is an accomplished song writer, conference and camp speaker, He and his wife, Janet, have three children.

THE REVELATION COURSE

It can be one of the most confusing books in the Bible, but it is also one of the most exciting books to study.

Join me in an in-depth look at this amazing book when you enroll in The Revelation Course.

Visit revelationcourse.com or my website patsieler.com to sign-up for more information

BIBLE BOOK SUMMARIES AND MORE

Have you visited PatSieler.com? On this site, I provide Bible book summaries, answers to your questions, and much more. Head over, sign-up to receive email notices of new posts. My purpose is to help you understand and apply the Bible to your life.

Thanks and God bless!.

STAY IN TOUCH!

I really appreciate you taking the time to read this book. I pray that God would use it to help you live a life totally dedicated to Him. I'd love to hear how it has helped you. I'd also love to hear any other comments you may have!

Let's stay in touch!
Send me an email: pat@patsieler.com
Friend me on Facebook:
facebook.com/patsielermedia
Follow me on Twitter: twitter.com/patsieler
Subscribe to my blog posts: patsieler.com